This book is dedicated to the MOST HIGH GOD 'ELOHIM'

The only TRUE GOD in my Life

Also our children whom we love very much

Nicole
Nikitha
Raphael
Emmanuel

www.iampublishers.co.uk

Divine Direction

'YOU'

Niina Nia Kabesa

www.iampublishers.co.uk

Printed June 2011

© 2011 Niina Nia Kabesa,

Published 2011 by IAM publishers

www.iampublishers.co.uk

ISBN 978-1-61364-299-3

All Bibles quotes are from
NKJV version unless stated otherwise!

TABLE OF CONTENTS

WELCOME!

www.iampublishers.co.uk

Now that you have crossed over, do not make the mistake many before you did. You need to start this walk alone with God first!

God will guide you on what to do and do not be Human's puppet because many will like to tell you how to be and what you should do.

Fear not, for the Lord is with you all the time and this book will not tell you what to do; it's a reflection on things we as Saint tend to overlook!

This book also will guide you on God's word, so that YOU will know for yourself who God is and what He wants to do in your life.

This book will also show you where you should go, now that you are born again!

Personal notes

_____
_____
_____
_____
_____
_____
_____
_____
_____
_____
_____
_____
_____
_____
_____
_____
_____
_____
_____
_____
_____
_____
_____
_____
_____
_____

8

Personal notes

Personal notes

Personal notes

WHO ARE YOU?

You are the most important individual in this Earth and according to *Genesis 1:31,* when God finished creating YOU in His image He saw that YOU looked <u>very</u> good (not just good, but <u>very</u>) which tells me, God liked YOU more than the rest of His creation because you are His child NOW!

In *Jeremiah 1:5* He said that He knows you before He formed YOU in your mother's womb! In other word your life in Christ is a pre-destined life.

YOU are in the beginning of a life which existed and was completed in the Spirit.

You are a spiritual being having a human being experience and no longer a human being having a spiritual being experience!

You are your environment! You are either living in the Kingdom of God or you are still living in the dirt!

When you are born again, you are royalty, you are part of the Kingdom of God and the devil is not happy about this!

That is why you must remain closer to God and let go of any old ways. It is very important that you find who you truly are in Christ and know that your salvation walk is an individual walk with God!

Believing and knowing are two different things, because in the Kingdom of God there are no fleshly conversations, only God's will for us!

Knowing who you are will help you in this journey, it will keep you focus on who you are with God and not who everyone else will want you to be.

Remember this walk is about you and God; as long as you keep doing this walk according to His ways, His will and His instructions, God will never leave you!

I believed in what I was doing when I was outside Christ and I did believe that I was a good person, but that did not stop people treating me bad, did it?

No matter how much I believed that I was a good person, without knowledge, I was like a car going around the roundabout; not knowing which turn to take after having taken many wrong turns!

When I got born again, it was until I closed myself away from the world that, I had a sense of knowing who I was in my new walk with Christ!

I stopped watching TV, I stood steel and paid attention to my environment and trained myself to identify the voices in my life! This is why I AM able to hear God's voice even in a chaotic or noisy environment.

Apart from God voice, I discovered that there were other voices which were dominating my life and I will discuss about the three stronger voices in the next chapter.

"To live your life based on other people's opinions is to not have a life! To consistently want to please others is to live a hypocritical life! Human have an insatiable appetite for blame. Noting you do will ever please them. Identify your shortcomings, apologies for your wrongs, settle with God, and end it there!!!!" © Unknown

Personal notes

_____
_____
_____
_____
_____
_____
_____
_____
_____
_____
_____
_____
_____
_____
_____
_____
_____
_____
_____
_____
_____
_____
_____
_____
_____

Personal notes

Personal notes

Personal notes

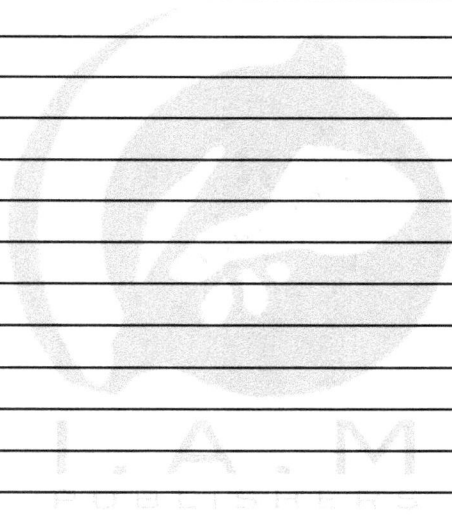

OTHER VOICES

I . A . M
PUBLISHERS

www.iampublishers.co.uk

To be aware of the voices which control your life is to be in line with your entire being. Here are the three powerful voices that I found were dictating and controlling my life:

TRADITION

This was one of the first voices that came up as I stood steel and away from the world. I found that even when I was away from the world, I still did act and believed certain ways, not because I was involved in tradition but because tradition is who I was.

i.e. when people tell me that they want to get married, I use to ask them first: 'have you seen the person's parents?' When what I really should have asked is: 'is it God will for your life?'

It is great to put our parents first, when it comes to the good news in our life but the first thing we should always do is seek God and let God be the first to always know everything. Even if we know that He knows, taking it to Him first shows that He is priority.

Tradition is there to carry on what was left behind from our forefathers, whom we know majority of them were idol worshipers.

PARENTAL

This was the second voice which came out of me.
I realized that most of the decision made in my previous life was due to my parent's advice and dictation on how my life ought to be. At time when parents say negative report of our lives unknown to us, we tend to fear to reject such confession. Our parent's will for our lives are not God's will for our lives.

 I'm very sure when Mary gave birth to Jesus, she wanted Him to get married and have children as any parent would for their child but, God will was that Jesus had to die on the cross and Mary accepted it! If you are from an African background, you will realize that this voice is a powerful voice over our lives and unless we train ourselves to identify these voices, we will never truly be walking in the fullness of the Lord because these voices have left an inprint in our mind!

SUBCONSCIENC

This is a voice which is easily ignored, yet very powerful to get rid of, because you do not identify it to anything as such. An example of how this voice work is as followed:

When you watch TV or listen to music, you will definitely forget about it in your mind when you go asleep, however your subconscious is like an Ocean full of hidden things. Everything that you do in your day to day life, whether you are consciously aware of them or not, they are stored in your subconscious. When you find yourself re-acting about someone behavior or irritated about how a person is behaving, this is an indication that you have a subconscious voice in you!

The only way out for you will be to deal with that area of your life and you'll see the change. This is one of the voices which I always tell my clients to be very careful about. If you do not stand steel to identify voices in your life, you will find it hard walking with Christ. That is why it is very *IM-PORTANT* that we as Saints apply *Roman 12:2* as a MUST!

Leaving as Saint is difficult and it is impossible if you are focus to the things of the world but possible when your focus is of the things of the Spirit of God. You will need the Holy Spirit to be working in you and through you for your walk to be easy here on earth.

That is why it is important for you to die in the flesh and let God's Spirit guide you. When you are born of the Spirit of God, serving Him is not an Obligation, rather a Natural thing to do or in my case your way of life!

Personal notes

Personal notes

Personal notes

Personal notes

WHERE DO YOU COME FROM?

I . A . M
PUBLISHERS

www.iampublishers.co.uk

This is a very difficult question to answer and I did struggle myself to answer this question. However, I did find a verse in the Bible which made it easier for me to understand this question!

1corinthians 7:20-23

"Let each one remain in the same calling in which he was called. Were you called while a slave? Do not be concerned about it; but if you can be made free, rather use it. For he who is called in the Lord while a slave is the Lord's freedman. Likewise he who is called while free is Christ's slave. You were bought at a price; do no become slaves of men."

You are either the Lords' Freedman or Christ Slave, what do I mean?

According to the revelation which I had in accordance to my own life, it was clear that being a freedman and a slave were two different things.

Before I could start explaining what this verse really means according to the revelation that the Lord gave me, we will look at the meaning of the words Freedman and Slave!

The Lord Freedman!

The word Freedman in dictionary.com means;
A man who has been freed from slavery,

Where you called while a slave? In other word, where you called while in sin? When many people hear the word slave, they almost always associate it with being chained and being whipped by some guard when you are working.

I lived a sinful life, I fornicated which resulted me to have 4 children out of wedlock. I am now aware that only God gives children as I have been told in Psalm 127v3 and I was a slave to sin because fornication was my way of life.

There is only one person who rules those who are living in sins, and that's Satan. You can be a born again Christian and still be living in sins, which many call backsliding. For me there is not such term as 'back slider', these blessed individuals are people who have such a higher calling in their lives. They are often dealing with a particular strong hold, living in denial or are not aware of the spiritual side of the salvation walk!

These are the type of individuals whom when they get freed of that which was controlling them, will become God Freedman/woman. These individuals should always listen to God and these individuals need to be lost in God and to avoid advice from other people, will be advisable until they feel that they are connected to God. The slave mentality will need to be removed and stay closer to God so that they will feel a sense of liberty.

These individuals are followers by nature but if they follow human, they will fall. They need to follow God and with God by their side they will become human leaders. That is why they are known to God has His freed man.

Christ Slave!

The word Slave in dictionary.com means;
1) A person who is the property of and wholly subject to another; a bond servant.
2) A person entirely under the domination of some influence or person: a slave to a drug.
3) To connect (a machine) to a master as its slave.

There were many other explanations to this word and I decided to explain these three as I was led by the spirit. When you do read the verse above you see that we are told not to be man slave but Christ's slave. You cannot become a slave of what you do not know or a master you have no knowledge of! When you do study the history of slavery you will notice one thing they all had in common about their master…RESPECT or some form of FEAR!

Many saints are lost today because they have no understanding of who God really is. They will quote the verse which tells us to worship Him in spirit and in truth but still build imagery about who God is. Many people will build alters in their homes and sometime it's a designated area in their house, which is for God alone failing to realize that He is a Spirit. What will happen when you are away from your alter and you needed something? Do you have to wait until you get back home?

This is just one amongst many tricks that the devil has planted in many saints today. We are to present our body to God as a sacrifice, which tells me that we are the temple of God. Wherever we go, we should still have the same spirit, character and attitude about God's ways. Being a slave to Christ simply means that we must believe in Him, connect with Him and fear Him. Everything which He taught us to do, we must do it with trembling fear.

Look onto God as your sole provider, protector, a friend in time of need. He will guide you according to the spirit and not in accordance of human ways. Change will not come straight away once you have been born again, your ability to act according to God's instruction and obedience will bring the supernatural change in your life!

CHOOSE TODAY WHO WILL YOU SERVE?

Personal notes

Personal notes

Personal notes

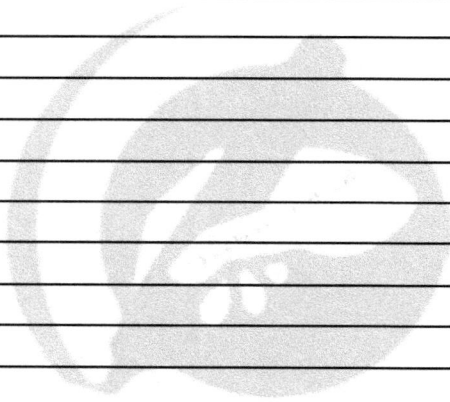

Personal notes

Personal notes

WHERE ARE YOU GOING?

"Also for Adam and his wife the Lord God made tunics of skin, and clothed them. Then the Lord God said, "Behold, the man has become like one of us, to know good and evil. And now, lest he put out his hand and take also of the tree of life, and eat, and live forever"- therefore the Lord God sent him out of the garden of Eden to till the ground from which he was taken. So He drove out the man; and He placed cherubim at the east of the Garden of Eden, and a flaming sword which turned every way, to guard the way to the tree of life"
Genesis 3: 21-24

What did happen in the garden was the cruellest thing that human ever did to God Right? Or is it similar to how every sinner lived life before they got born again?

When you read the verse you see that even though they sinned against God, it was God who made their garment and it was God who dressed them. Why did He not reject them or even thru them in HELL? Where was HELL and when was it CREATED?

Apply this in your life now that you are born again, know that all you went through God saw and regardless of what it was He knew you will be here one day and you have made it.

Adam and eve had no clue what their lives were going to be; in fact they had no clue of what they were going to do after the fall. God being a good God all the time made a dress for them and dress them and place them to another place where they could live. God did not abandon them because they failed Him, nor did He walk away from them. He told them off and removed them from the Garden of Eden simply because He was protecting the tree of Eternal life! However, that was not just the only reason; God realised that the human became like THEM by knowing the good and bad!

This simply means that as a born again Christian you have a one plus that many in the world do not have. You are guarantee of eternal Life, while many people and their powers are limited.

Human already are like God because they know good and evil, but God has the key to eternal life and that is what you will have when you become born again and grow to know God personally!

Adam and eve did not know where they were going after the fall, they just trusted whatever God was doing was going to work for them, and they knew however that the consequence of their sins was going to be paid.

Just like you, when you are born again, coming from a sinful life into God palace, unlike Adam and Eve, you have not been kicked out but have been invited into the Garden, which is the atmosphere of God!

Adam and eve could not go back to the paradise, that's why God in Christ came to give you the access through Jesus Christ to come back. You are not going anywhere but to the Kingdom of abba father.

So let no one tell you any other way other than when you are born again, you are and have been called to be at the garden. Start working out your salvation to get back there and it starts by knowing God's word for your life.

However before you get to the paradise, there are things which you must put in place and they are as follow:

Where do you want to be?

The Bible made it clear in **Colossians 1:16** "*For by Him all things were created that are in heaven and that are on earth, visible and invisible, whether thrones or dominions or principalities or powers. ALL THINGS WERE CREATED THROUGH HIM AND FOR HIM.*"

When you got asked where you want to be, it means that you have a choice to be God creation or God's child. Is it safe to say that Satan was created THROUGH GOD, FOR GOD and NOT YOU? The verse above states that all which was created by God are God's not ours. If that's the case, then why do YOU FIGHT Satan? I did not write these words in the bible God did.

Moving on, now we know that all creation was created THROUGH GOD and FOR GOD. Does this mean that all are God children? NO! Heaven NO!

"But as many as received Him, to them He gave the right to become children of God, to those who believe in His name: who were born, not of blood, nor of the will of the flesh, nor of the will of man, but of God." **John 1:12-13**

"For as many as are led by the Spirit of God, these are sons of God." **Romans 8:14**

"To redeem those who were under the law, that we might receive the adoption as sons. And because you are sons, God has sent forth the Spirit of His Son into your hearts, crying out, 'Abba, Father!' Therefore you are no longer a slave but a son, and if a son, then an heir of God through Christ" **Galatians 4:5-7**

Why should we love sinners if they are not God children?

"But God demonstrates His own love toward us, in that while we were still sinners, Christ died for us." **Roman5:8**

Remember that God only came to earth through Christ to save the sinners, therefor when we are born again, we are God's children and we **MUST** do what He came to do.

Are you grounded in God enough to turn sinners to Christ without preaching?

Do you know that there are many preachers in this world, than there were back in the days of Jesus?

Amongst these preachers, many no longer operate with the Holy Spirit because they have reason to believe that the other God they are worshiping is better than OUR JEHOVAH!

If you look closely on what did happen in the Garden, you will see that the only person that was preaching was Satan, while God was instructing and teaching!

In the dictionary.com to teach means: To impart knowledge of or skill in; give instruction in; to impart knowledge or skill to; give instruction to;

While the word to preach means:

To deliver a sermon; to give Ernest advice, as a religious or moral subjects or the like; to advocate or inculcate (religious or moral truth, right conduct, etc.) in speech or writing;

When Satan did approach eve, he was probably telling her: 'Look, I have been around God for a while, are you really sure that's what you heard?' and often that's what Human/flesh do to the Spirit, always questioning instead of understanding that God is a God who teaches, instruct and that's that!

Does your life style reflect God purity and righteousness?

A daily study of who God is and reading the bible will often help you to walk in the fullness of His glory. If I was to give an example of what I did, is that I closed myself away from all the things that I used to love and gave God 100% of my time.

This was beneficial to me and as time went by, I started loving God presences even more and realised that there were devices which the devil do use to distract the children of God and I will talk about them in my other books. Purity and righteousness is the walk which will make the devil and his demon flee from you.

What will you do when you get there?

Adam and eve knew what they had to do when they got to the place where God place them. What about us who are born again? We go back to the palace; however do you know what you will do when you get there?

"Then God blessed them, and God said to them, "Be fruitful and multiply; fill the earth and subdue it; have dominion over the fish of the sea, over the birds of the air, and over every living thing that moves on the earth." And God said, "See, I have given you every herb that yields seed which is on the face of all the earth, and every tree whose fruit yields seed; to you it shall be for food. Also, to every beast of the earth, to every bird of the air, and to everything that creeps on the earth, in which there is life, I have given every green herb for food"; and it was so. Then God saw everything that He had made, and indeed it was very good. So the evening and the morning were the sixth day." Genesis 1:28-31

As a new creature, we must know that being born again means that you are back in the garden; this is something many churches will not talk about because they got everyone focused on Satan being bad instead of talking about God's plans all the time.

We were not created for the devil but God, the devil is God's business not yours as the scripture in *Colossians 1:16* says *"For by Him all things were created that are in heaven and that are on earth, visible and invisible, whether thrones or dominions or principalities or powers. ALL THINGS WERE CREATED THROUGH HIM AND FOR HIM."*

You cannot touch anything unless God himself allows it. When you speak of a person or your focus is on something most of the time, that thing or person becomes your GOD!

SO when many are talking about the bad which the devil does, we are not and I repeat NOT, Glorifying GOD! This is the BIGEST trick which is in our churches today. Knowledge comes from the Lord and I will rather speak of God goodness all the days of my life, regardless of my circumstance. God does not want the devil back in the Garden, so when you are always focusing on what the devil is doing, you are forgetting that in the Bible it was God Himself who gave the devil permission to test His children!

SO again I say unto thee, it is not the devil in your life that you should worry about! It is God whom you need to go to in every circumstance, and ask; 'what should I do, what wrong did I do and can I fix this Lord?' THAT'S IT!

So before you think of having that warfare please pray to God and ask God to send you people who are spiritually strong to carry it for you. This is another area which is missing in our churches today but I will talk about it in my next 'DD edition –Churches'!

These are what I call the dying of the Human flesh, the end of the wilderness or the battle between the spirit and the flesh. Having an understanding of the Lord will make you a walking spirit, and no longer a fleshly individual, because we are told in *1corinthians 1:29* *"that no flesh should glory in His presence".* BUT, when the transformation has taken place, here are the BIGGEST steps which will follow:

God will test your faith

There are verses from the Bible teaching you that God allow certain amount of trials and tribulations to come your way in this life, but He also uses some of these trials as a way of actually testing us from time to time!

One of the areas that God will arrange for a test to come your way in this life will be when you are getting ready to walk into the heart of your true calling for Him. This was a definite pattern of God in both the Old and New Testaments of the Bible. If God is calling you to be a great pastor, a great Bible teacher, or a great evangelist, rest assured that you will have a big test coming your way right at the point that you are getting ready to walk into that calling.

When this test does come your way, it is important that you take this test very seriously, as it will determine whether or not God will actually promote and release you into your true calling for Him. Fail this test and you will either lose the call all together, or you will cause a major delay to occur as to when you will be actually released to move into that calling.

I will give you 4 very powerful examples from the Bible where God did this with 4 different people, with one of the tests actually being done to His very own Son, Jesus Christ.

If God tested His own Son with a specific test, rest assured that He will test each one of you if you have a specific type of calling in His perfect plan for your life. Study and meditate on these 4 dramatic examples from the Bible very carefully, as each one of these tests was very severe and very trying for the actual people involved.

The reason why God is going to test you before your big, final breakthrough in Him is because He has to see if you got what it takes to actually make the grade in that specific calling for Him.

He will test your BOLDNESS out like they do in the army with all of their recruits. Pass this test and you will be finally promoted into God's best for your life. Fail this test and you will either lose the call all together and then be forced to settle for God's plan B for your life or you will be dismiss and set further back until you are ready to pass this kind of test at a later date.

I will be talking in the next chapter about the 4 very powerful and dramatic tests that God had arranged for some of His people to pass back in both the Old and New Testaments in the Bible.

Personal notes

Personal notes

Personal notes

Personal notes

Personal notes

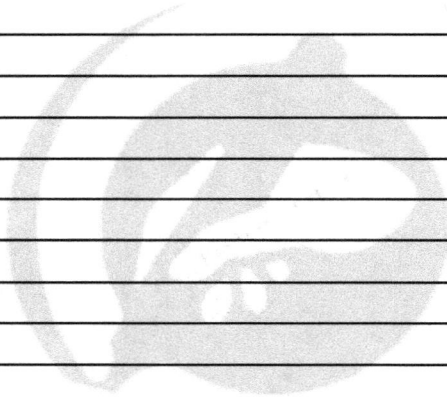

SPECIFIC TESTS FROM GOD

1. **Obedience**

This test was given to Abraham in the Book of Genesis.

Most of you have heard of this test. God asked Abraham to put his son Isaac on an altar and then asked him to take a knife and kill his own son. As we all know, Abraham went as far as to actually tie his son down to the altar and had the knife in his hand ready to strike down on him to take his life, when God suddenly sent an angel down to stop him.

How many of us could actually pass such an extreme test today, especially in the type of world we now live in where you would be immediately prosecuted if you even tried to do such a thing. I personally do not think God would ever do this type of test in our current day and age due to the extreme dangers of it. But the point to get is that God may actually arrange for a test to occur to test your actual loyalty and obedience to Him. It is important that we fully obey every order and directive that we receive from the Lord in this life. If we cannot be fully obedient to the specific commands and leadings of the Holy Spirit, then God will not be able to use us in the actual callings that He has set up for our lives.

In the world we live in, this test will actually be hard for many to pass. The reason being is due to the material and lustful things that are out there competing for our time and attention. These material things will cause our flesh to want to try and act up and once our flesh has been disturb, it will do everything it can to try and get its own way, even if it means disobeying God Himself. That is why God will test you in this specific area to see if you will have the strength and character in your personality to be able to override the desires of your flesh and ego, and be willing to obey God over all of your wants and desires for these material and lustful objects.

God will know where your deep veins and weak spots will be on these kinds of tests, so He will probably arrange for these types of tests to target some of your weak and vulnerable spots, just like He did with Abraham by asking him to sacrifice his one and only son at the time that this test was being set up. God may ask you to give something or someone up. He may ask you to give up the job you are currently working at, or the person you are currently dating, as this person may not be the one that He has personally picked out to be your mate in this life. But whatever God may be asking you to do for Him, realize that this is an obedience test being sent your way, and you must fully obey the Lord with whatever He will be asking you to do for Him. If you do not obey His specific directive and you choose to follow your own desires and your own wants on these kinds of issues, then God will not be able to use you in the specific calling that He has set up for your life.

If you can't or won't obey God with this specific command, then God will question and doubt your ability to fully obey Him further on down the road with anything else that He may be asking you to do for Him. Bottom line – God is our Shepherd and we as His sheep are to fully follow Him in this life and every single directive and command that He will be giving us along the way. The Bible tells us that we are to be led by the Holy Spirit in this life – not by our own wants and desires or even worse by other people's theories of our life.

This test will determine who gets promoted into their true callings in the Lord and who does not. Abraham passed his test and you saw what happened to him as a result. He became the father of many nations and his bloodline was used as the bloodline that brought our Saviour Jesus Christ into our world so He could go to the cross and save all of us from our sins.

Here is the verse that will tell you what the consequence were as a result of Abraham perfectly obeying the voice of God on being willing to sacrifice his son Isaac: *"In your seed all the nations of the earth shall be blessed, because you have OBEYED MY voice."* **Genesis 22:18**

If you want to enter into your true calling in the Lord, you need to get it settled right now in your mind and in your heart that you will fully obey the Lord with every specific thing that He will be asking you to do for Him in this life. Imagine if Abraham did say "that voice could not be of the Lord, why would God give me a child and now He asks me to kill him again?" This happens often to believer because we fail to understand that GOD is GOD, HE can do whatever HE wants with us, however HE chooses too. If you can agree to do things God's way rather than your own way in this life, then you will be promoted into God's best for your life, and you can then proceed to leave your mark in this world in the specific calling that He will be setting up for your life.

2. **Patience**

This is where you have done everything you have been asked to do, but now God is going to ask you to just sit and wait for the big breakthrough to occur. A perfect example of this type of trying test in the Bible is the story of Moses and the parting of the Red Sea. When Moses rescue and deliver the Israelites from the Egyptians, he then brought them before the Red Sea with nowhere else to go or turn to. The Promised Land is in the other side, but there is no way they can reach it unless God first parts the Red Sea.

What does God do next? Instead of immediately parting the Red Sea for all of them to get to the other side, He causes all of them to sit and wait for a while before He actually parts the Red Sea. The children of Israel cannot move forward or else they will drown in the Red Sea. They cannot go backwards or else they will fall back into slavery with the Egyptians, as the Egyptians are now starting to come back after them. They have no other choice but to just sit and wait for God to part the Red Sea.

The Bible does not say how long God made them wait before He parted the Red Sea but we know it was long enough to really try their patience, as many of them started complaining to Moses about it. Some of them even went as far as stating they wanted to go back to Egypt, as they at least had food and shelter under the Egyptian rule. This type of test could occur to some of you right before your big breakthrough with the Lord. What you will have to do is override your flesh and your own impatience and simply rely on God's peace through the Holy Spirit and God's perfect timing as to when He will want to open up that door for you.

If you ever find yourself facing this kind of trying test, make sure that you do not let your impatience get the better of you and cause you to walk away from that door that you are sitting in front of – as that door could be opening up at any-time. Stay put right where God has you currently at and force your-self to wait until that door either opens up for you to walk through, or God tells you to do something different. Again, what would have happened in this story of Moses if they would not have waited for God to part that Red Sea? What would have happened to the Jewish people as a nation and as a people if they would have gone back into slavery with the Egyptians, if they would not have waited for this miraculous event to occur with the Lord? The course of Jewish history could have been completely changed and altered forever if Moses would not have had enough patience to wait for God to part that Red Sea.

Your life is like a chessboard to the Lord. He is the One who will be making all of the major chess moves on your chess board. Not only must you fully rely on God to make these chess moves in your life, but you must also rely on His perfect timing as to when He will be making all of these specific chess moves. One wrong move or one move made at the wrong time could cause your whole call in God to completely unravel and fall apart.

3. <u>Faith and Belief</u>

This is where God will be showing you what is on the other side of your true calling in Him. When God does this, He may show you what some of the obstacles, roadblocks and opposition may end up being. He may show you exactly what you will have to face. This is where you will be shown all of the Goliaths and strongholds that you may have to face and engage with once you cross over into the actual calling.

A perfect example of this type of test has to be with what God did with the children of Israel just after He had got done rescuing them from the Egyptians in the story of Moses. Shortly after delivering them from the Egyptians, He brought them right up to their Promised Land. But instead of sending all of them immediately in, He sends in only 12 spies so they could first spy out the land so they could see exactly what they were going to have to face once they actually entered into this land. And what happens next?

10 of the spies come back with a bad report. They come back telling the rest of the people that the people who dwell there were "strong," that many of the cities were "fortified," that it was a land that devoured its inhabitants, that all of the men they saw were of "great stature," and that they were like grasshoppers in the face of these types of "giants." However, Joshua and Caleb, who were 2 of the 12 spies, came back with a different report. The saw the exact same things the other 10 spies saw, but they had a completely different outlook and perspective about it. They had just seen God miraculously deliver them from the Egyptian rule, so they knew God would have no problems in taking out the giants and strongholds they saw in this Promised Land.

As a result of these other 10 spies coming back with this bad report, this kindled the anger of God and caused Him to then pronounce a very severe judgment on all of them. He told these 10 spies that they and all of the other men over 20 years of age would not enter into this Promised Land. He said they would all wander in the desert for the next 40 years where they would then all eventually die out there.

Since Joshua and Caleb had a different spirit about them and fully believed that God could take out all of these giants and strongholds, He tells them that both of them and all of the people under 20 years of age would be the ones who would be allowed to enter into the Promised Land – all because they had enough courage, faith and belief in the Lord that He could give them the victories once they had crossed over and started to possess parts of the land that He wanted them to have for themselves. Plain and simple, this was a faith and belief test. God showed them exactly what was waiting for them on the other side and the test was – can they believe in God and His supernatural power to defeat the enemies and strongholds they would have to directly face – or will they want to turn around and go back into the desert, never giving God a chance to show them what He could miraculously do for them?

As we all know, these 10 spies failed this test not only for themselves, but for the rest of the men and woman over 20 years of age. In the same way, God could test some of you with this same type of test. He will show you exactly what will be awaiting you on the other side once you cross over into your true calling for Him. He will show you the opposition, the giants, the strongholds, and the points of resistance you will have to directly face. He will then sits back and watch your reaction to all of it. Will you fully believe that He can conquer and overcome all of these obstacles and roadblocks for you, or will you get scared and lose faith and belief in Him that He can overcome all of the roadblocks and obstacles that you are seeing?

All of the Israelites 20 years and older in the above story lost their one and only chance to enter into the Promised land – all simply because they could not work up enough faith and belief in the Lord to fully conquer and over-come all of the points of opposition and resistance they initially saw.

If you are ever faced with this kind of a severe test with the Lord, you will have to make a very big decision one way or the other. You will either have to fully believe that God is calling you to go through this door, and that He will then anoint you with His power to be victorious in this calling – or you will let fear and intimidation get the better of you and you will then walk out on the call that God has set up for your life.

Joshua and Caleb ended up going into the Promised Land after the 40 years was up and the Bible says that Joshua was able to conquer and gain full pos-session of every ounce of land that his foot had stepped on – all because he had enough faith and belief in God that He could do this for him. If God is no respecter of persons and He was able to do this for Joshua and the rest of the Jewish people in this story, then God can do the exact same thing for every born-again believer who will fully surrender to His call on their lives and then be willing to have enough faith and belief in Him to enter into that call and take on all of the opposition and roadblocks they will end up facing down the road in that calling.

4. <u>Sin</u>

This test is exactly what God did with His Son Jesus. After Jesus gets baptized with the Holy Spirit in the Jordan River; God does something strange with Jesus, instead of sending Jesus right of way into His three and half year miracle ministry and then to the cross to save all of us, God sends His Son out into the desert to face a temptation test direct with the devil himself.

Why would God send His Son Jesus out in the desert to let the devil tempt Him with three specific temptations, knowing full well that He was going to pass this test anyway and if He wanted to test Him, why this kind of a specific test? The reason God tested His Son Jesus with this temptation test was because He had to see if Jesus would have fallen for any of these specific temptations by the devil. If He would have fallen for any one of them, He would have sinned against God the Father and if He would have committed so much as one sin against His Father, then He would not have been able to go to the cross to save any of us.

One of the conditions of Jesus being able to go to the cross in human flesh form for all of us was that He had to be perfectly sin-free. One sin would have totally disqualified Him and He then would not have been able to go to the cross for all of us. Part of the conditions for this ultimate sacrifice for all of us was that it had to be a "perfect" sacrifice, which meant that Jesus had to be perfect in His human flesh form, meaning that He had to be completely sin-free. That was why God had to specifically test Him on this issue, to see if He would fall and commit at least one sin. As we all know, Jesus passed this test with flying colours and the Bible says that He did not commit so much as one sin when He walked among us for those 33 years. As a result of not committing any sins, Jesus was perfectly qualified to go to the cross for all of us.

In the same way, God may test some of you with this same kind of a sin test. The reason being is that He will want to test your resolve to stay out of any type of serious sin. Adultery, fornication, bribery, and the hunger and love for money could all lead to your ruin once you cross over into your true calling in the Lord. Look how many modern day ministries have been brought down by adultery, fornication, and the misuse of money and funds! Just as God allowed Adam and Eve to be tested in the Garden of Eden and His own Son Jesus to be tested in a desert setting with the devil, God may allow some of you to be tested on this same kind of issue.

Pass this sin test and do not succumb to any demonic temptations, and you will then be trusted by the Lord, and He will then promote you into your true calling for Him. Fail these tests, and you could completely lose your entire calling in the Lord, just like Adam and Eve managed to do in the Garden of Eden. If by chance this kind of a test ever comes your way, take it very seriously, as there may not be any second chances for you if you fail this kind of a test. This one is very serious. If Jesus would have fallen for any one of those three specific temptations from the devil, He would have completely lost His entire calling in God and He then would not have been able to go to the cross to save any of us. In the same way, you could lose your entire call in God if you succumb to any of these temptations. There is obviously always full forgiveness and full restoration for you with the Lord if you confess and repent of these sins, but what you could lose is that open door into the heart of your true call for Him due to the consequences that may result from you falling into a heavier type of sin. Many major men of God have never been able to get back their big, huge, successful TV ministries once they lost them due to falling into these types of heavier sins.

In conclusion, if you will notice in the above 4 examples, these were all deal-breaking tests. When the tests were passed, these people then went into the heart of their true calls with the Lord. When they were flunked, like the children of Israel managed to do with God the Father on the Promised Land issue, they completely lost the divine destinies that God had originally set up for all of them to walk into.

That is why these tests should be taken seriously if you ever happen to have one of them come your way. These types of tests can also be brought your way by the Lord at any time during your life's journey with Him. From time to time, the Bible says that the Lord will test the righteous. When these types of tests do come your way, make sure that you see them for what they are and do your best to pass them with flying colours. If you do, then God will continue to bring you up higher in your divine destiny with Him. Fail these tests or do poorly with them, and God may have to hold you back for a while until you can see what He is trying to teach you and show you.

Besides the above 4 types of tests could be other types of tests. Some of you could be tested on your ability to forgive what others may have done to hurt you in your past. The Bible is very clear in that we have to forgive everyone who has ever trespassed against us and if we do not, then God will not forgive us of our own trespasses. If you cannot get your own personal sins forgiven with the Lord, then you may have a very hard time in walking out your true call with Him since it will obviously damage your personal relationship with Him.

I hope these 4 tests will serve as good heads-up for any of you who will either face this kind of testing in your near future, or if by chance you are already in the middle of this type of testing right now due to the closeness of entering into your true calling in the Lord.

God bless you and welcome to God's world

Personal notes

Personal notes

Personal notes

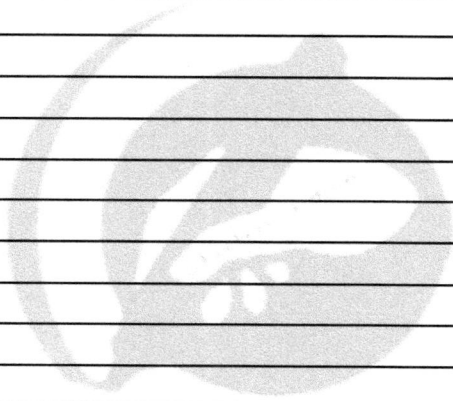

Personal notes

Personal notes

Personal notes

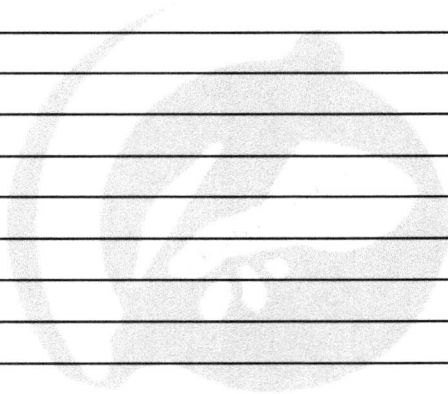

Personal notes

Personal notes

ABOUT THE AUTHORS

www.monniinskabesa.co.uk
www.godilisious.com

The young author has a passion for God and she is after God's Heart. She wants to accomplish her call here on earth according to God will for her!

If you choose to support the young lady's ministry please visit www.heaveneyes.co.uk and make your contribution.

God bless you all!

-